中国法院知识产权
司法保护状况

2022年

Intellectual Property Protection by
Chinese Courts in 2022

最高人民法院知识产权审判庭　编

人民法院出版社

图书在版编目（CIP）数据

中国法院知识产权司法保护状况. 2022年 / 最高人民法院知识产权审判庭编. -- 北京：人民法院出版社，2023.5

ISBN 978-7-5109-3794-1

Ⅰ．①中… Ⅱ．①最… Ⅲ．①知识产权保护－研究－中国－2022 Ⅳ．①D923.404

中国国家版本馆CIP数据核字(2023)第077425号

中国法院知识产权司法保护状况（2022年）

最高人民法院知识产权审判庭　编

责任编辑	丁丽娜
出版发行	人民法院出版社
地　　址	北京市东城区东交民巷27号（100745）
电　　话	（010）67550608（责任编辑）　　67550558（发行部查询）
	65223677（读者服务部）
客服QQ	2092078039
网　　址	http://www.courtbook.com.cn
E‐mail	courtpress@sohu.com
印　　刷	北京瑞禾彩色印刷有限公司
经　　销	新华书店
开　　本	787毫米×1092毫米　1/16
字　　数	55千字
印　　张	4.5
版　　次	2023年5月第1版　2023年5月第1次印刷
书　　号	ISBN 978-7-5109-3794-1
定　　价	28.00元

版权所有　侵权必究

目　录

前　言 ·· 1

一、充分发挥审判职能，服务创新驱动发展 ······················· 2

二、激励保障科技创新，促进科技自立自强 ······················· 5

三、加强商标司法保护，助推品牌培育发展 ······················· 7

四、强化著作权审判，服务文化强国建设 ··························· 9

五、维护竞争法治环境，激发创新创造活力 ····················· 11

六、深入推进司法改革，提升整体保护效能 ····················· 13

七、坚持依法平等保护，促进国际交流合作 ····················· 17

八、发挥党建引领作用，锻造一流审判队伍 ····················· 18

结束语 ··· 20

附件：2022年全国法院新收知识产权案件类型与数量图 ············ 21

CONTENTS

Introduction 25

I. Fully Utilizing Trial Functions to Support Innovation-
   Driven Development 26
II. Encouraging and Assuring Scientific and Technological
    Innovation to Promote Self-reliance and Strength 32
III. Increasing Judicial Protection of Trademarks to
     Enable the Growth of Successful Brands 37
IV. Strengthening Copyright Trials to Contribute to the
    Building of a Country with a Strong Culture 41
V. Maintaining a Sound Legal Environment for
   Competition to Stimulate Innovation and Creativity 44
VI. Deepening Judicial Reforms to Improve Efficiency and
    Quality of IP rights Protection 48
VII. Upholding the Legal Equality in IP rights Protection and
     Promoting International Communication and Cooperation 58
VIII. Leveraging the Guiding Role of Party Building to
      Build a First-Class Judicial Team 60

Conclusion 63

特别说明：

《中国法院知识产权司法保护状况（2022年）》以中英两种文本发布，以中文文本为准。

Special Remarks:

This paper is published in both Chinese and English. The Chinese version shall be the authoritative version for interpretation purposes.

中国法院知识产权司法保护状况
（2022 年）

前　言

　　党的二十大报告强调实现高质量发展是中国式现代化的本质要求之一，明确坚持创新在我国现代化建设全局中的核心地位，并专门就加强知识产权法治保障作出部署。2022 年，人民法院坚持以习近平新时代中国特色社会主义思想为指导，全面贯彻落实党的二十大精神，深入贯彻习近平法治思想，心怀国之大者，紧紧围绕"努力让人民群众在每一个司法案件中感受到公平正义"目标，增强做好新时代知识产权审判工作的责任感使命感，推动知识产权司法保护水平不断提升。

一、充分发挥审判职能，服务创新驱动发展

2022年，人民法院着力强化审判职能作用，依法公正高效审理各类知识产权案件，新收一审、二审、申请再审等各类知识产权案件526165件，审结543379件（含旧存，下同），比2021年分别下降18.17%和9.67%。

地方各级人民法院新收知识产权民事一审案件438480件，审结457805件，比2021年分别下降20.31%和11.25%。其中，新收专利案件38970件，同比上升23.25%；商标案件112474件，同比下降9.82%；著作权案件255693件，同比下降29.07%；技术合同案件4238件，同比上升5.55%；竞争类案件9388件，同比上升11.51%；其他知识产权民事纠纷案件17717件，同比下降15.66%。地方各级人民法院新收知识产权民事二审案件46524件，审结46563件，同比分别下降5.22%和上升2.41%。最高人民法院新收知识产权民事案件3786件，审结3073件，比2021年分别下降10.77%和13.61%。

地方各级人民法院新收知识产权行政一审案件20634件，审结17630件，比2021年分别上升0.35%和下降8.85%。其中，新收专利案件1876件，同比上升3.65%；商标案件18738件，比2021年增加4件；著作权案件12件，比2021年减少7件；其他案件8件。地方各级人民法院新收知识产权行政二审案件5897件，审结7285件，比2021年分别下降28.22%和1.79%。其中，维持原判5518件，改判1650件，发回重审3件，撤诉78件，驳回起诉10件，其

他 26 件。最高人民法院新收知识产权行政案件 1456 件，审结 1542 件，比 2021 年分别下降 48.95% 和 38%。

地方各级人民法院新收侵犯知识产权刑事一审案件 5336 件，审结 5456 件，比 2021 年分别下降 14.98% 和 9.76%。其中，新收侵犯注册商标类刑事案件 4971 件，审结 5099 件，同比下降 15.3% 和 9.86%；新收侵犯著作权类刑事案件 304 件，审结 302 件，同比下降 8.71% 和 7.93%；新收其他刑事案件 61 件，审结 55 件，比 2021 年减少 13 件和 6 件。地方各级人民法院新收涉知识产权的刑事二审案件 979 件，审结 977 件，同比分别下降 6.76% 和 2.01%。

2022 年，人民法院受理的知识产权案件呈现以下主要特点。

技术类案件数量持续上升，中西部等地知识产权保护需求强劲，知识产权司法服务高质量发展作用进一步凸显。2022 年，最高人民法院知识产权法庭新收技术类知识产权民事二审实体案件数量保持较高增长。地方各级人民法院新收涉专利、技术合同一审案件数量增幅明显。江苏法院新收技术性较强的知识产权权属、侵权纠纷案件 1817 件，同比增长 17.61%。山西、海南法院新收知识产权案件数量同比增长达 22.21% 和 72.58%。河北法院知识产权案件收结案数同比增长 45.94% 和 106.01%。辽宁法院新收知识产权民事案件数同比增长 61%。江西法院新收知识产权民事一审案件数同比增长 22%。湖南、黑龙江、新疆生产建设兵团等地法院收案量也延续了稳定增长的态势。

知识产权案件互联网审判机制不断创新，智慧法院建设深入推进，司法便民利民机制持续健全。各地法院依托互联网审判平台，全面开展知识产权案件线上庭审、送达等工作，有效缩短诉讼周期，降低诉讼成本。上海法院全年知识产权案件线上立案38505件，组织在线开庭、谈话等2万余场，电子送达超17万次。河南法院知识产权一审案件网上立案16023件，网上立案率超90%。青海法院知识产权案件网上立案率达62.7%，通过送达平台电子送达898次。广西贵港中院利用数字赋能，全年网上立案量约占全部受理知识产权案件的70%。青岛知识产权法庭建设互联网异步质证系统，当事人在线上传电子化证据材料完成质证，庭前程序更加高效便捷。

纠纷实质性化解持续加强，权利人权益保障更加全面，人民群众知识产权司法获得感日益增强。 2022年，全国法院知识产权民事一审案件调解结案44155件，调解结案率9.64%，比2021年增加0.78个百分点。知识产权民事二审案件解调结案2894件，调解结案率6.22%，比2021年增加0.57个百分点。天津法院知识产权民事一审案件调撤率达75.51%。河北法院知识产权案件调撤率达73.48%。广东法院知识产权民事一审案件调撤率为52.94%。黑龙江法院全年知识产权案件总体调撤率达66.6%。当事人诉累有效减轻，社会和谐稳定得到充分维护。江苏法院审理适用惩罚性赔偿的知识产权案件97件，同比增长21.25%。上海浦东法院全年审理25件适用惩罚性赔偿知识产权案件。深圳中院在29件知识产权案件中适用惩罚性赔偿，累计判赔金额达1.69亿元。湖南法院开展专项行动，执结涉知识产权案件3796件，执行到位金额6043.15万元。广东法院不到20%的知识产权民事案件进入强制执行，执行案件结收比约98%。江苏法院针对涉食品、药品等重点民生领域侵犯知识产权犯罪行为，发放"从业禁止令"近百份。贵州贵阳中院全年办理知识产权财产保全案件 25 件，依申请查封、冻结财产 4010 万元。知识产权侵权违法成本显著提高，权利人损失得到有效弥补。

审判重心有序下沉，中级、高级法院管辖分工更加完善，知识产权案件审判质效稳步提升。2022 年，江苏基层法院知识产权案件受理数占全省知识产权案件总数的 65.25%，同比上升 10.52 个百分点，中级法院和高级法院案件受理数占比减少至 31.56% 和 3.19%。重庆基层法院新收知识产权案件数占全市知识产权案件总数的 75.2%，同比增长 28.1 个百分点；中级法院占 21.3%，同比下降 29.9 个百分点；高级法院占 3.5%，同比增长 1.8 个百分点。知识产权案件审理"金字塔"格局逐步形成。地方各级人民法院审结的知识产权民事一审案件中，有 320 件结案方式为上级法院提级管辖，数量是 2021 年的 3 倍多。江西法院全年提级审理 63 件知识产权民事一审案件，广东法院全年提级审理 15 件新类型、疑难复杂或者具有法律适用指导意义的知识产权案件，有效促进裁判规则统一。

二、激励保障科技创新，促进科技自立自强

加快实现高水平科技自立自强，是推动高质量发展的必由之路。人民法院充分发挥知识产权审判对科技创新的激励和保障作用，通过高质量知识产权司法，支持基础研究，保障原创性引领性科技攻关，打通制约推进高质量发展的卡点瓶颈。

（一）持续推动技术类案件裁判标准统一

人民法院以强化保护为导向，加强对专利授权确权行政行为合法性的严格审查，推动行政标准与司法标准统一，促进专利授权确权质量提升。充分发挥司法裁判在科技创新成果保护中的规则引领和价值导向功能，总结提炼司法保护新规则，促进技术和产业不断创新升级。2022年，最高人民法院合理定位四级法院审判职能，明确发明专利、实用新型专利、植物新品种、集成电路布图设计、技术秘密、计算机软件的权属、侵权纠纷案件由知识产权法院、省会城市中级法院和最高人民法院确定的中级法院集中管辖，有效促进全国技术类案件裁判标准统一，提升重大科技创新的司法保障水平。发布上一年度中国法院10大知识产权案件和50件典型知识产权案例，其中包括11件技术类案件，分别涉及侵害技术秘密、侵害植物新品种权、侵害发明专利权等，有效指导审判实践。对《关于审理申请注册的药品相关的专利权纠纷民事案件适用法律若干问题的规定》等司法解释的实施情况进行调研，及时总结案件审判经验。最高人民法院审理"气化炉除尘装置及系统"专利权权属案，合理界定技术来源方和技术改进方获得权利的基础。审理齐鲁制药与四环制药专利无效行政纠纷案，明确药品专利创造性和说明书充分公开的判断标准。审理"整体式土工格室"侵害实用新型专利权纠纷案，明确合法来源抗辩中是否尽到合理注意义务的审查思路。

（二）着力服务保障基础研究及原始创新

人民法院立足"四个面向"，加强关键领域、核心技术、新兴产业知识产权司法保护，维护创新主体合法权益，服务保障打赢关键核心技术攻坚战。最高人民法院深入贯彻落实党中央关于种业振兴决策部署，与农业农村部等部门联合印发《关于保护种业知识产权打击假冒伪劣套牌侵权营造种业振兴良好环境的指导意见》，发布第二批人民法院种业知识产权司法保护典型案例10件，支持设立人民法院知识产权司法保护种质资源研究（海南）基地并首次以基地名义召开种质资源知识产权司法保护研讨会。审理的"金粳818"水稻品种侵权案入选"新时代推动法治进程2021年度十大案件"。审结全国首例药品专利链接诉讼案，推动药品专利链接制度落地完善，入选"新时代推动法治进程2022年度十大提名案件"。在两起"蜜胺"专利及技术秘密侵权关联案件中，判令各被告连带赔偿权利人经济损失合计2.18亿元，切实体现大力保护科技创新的司法导向。审理"油气微生物勘探"技术秘密侵权案，释放加强技术秘密保护的强烈信号。江苏高院与省有关部门围绕知识产权助力产业强链和自主可控现代产业体系建设签署备忘录，建立服务重点产业链发展工作机制。苏州知识产权法庭在涉美国公司侵害发明专利权纠纷案中促成当事双方达成一揽子和解，有力维护创新主体合法权益。合肥知识产权法庭与行政执法机关及省内企业座谈，听取回应市场创新主体维权需求。

三、加强商标司法保护，助推品牌培育发展

人民法院持续加强商标权司法保护，不断提高商标授权确权行政案件和商标民事案件审理质量，维护商标申请注册及使用秩序，

引导权利人依法申请注册并规范使用商标,坚决维护市场法治环境,助力新时代品牌强国建设。

（一）提升商标授权确权质量

提高商标授权确权行政案件审理质量,坚决打击不以使用为目的的商标恶意注册行为,科学合理界定商标权权利边界与保护范围,促进商标申请注册秩序正常化和规范化。最高人民法院与国家知识产权局开展座谈,征集全国法院意见,为商标法修改、地理标志立法等法律修改制定工作提供高质量建议参考,推动商标类法规制度不断健全,商标授权确权规则更加完善。最高人民法院审结的"陈麻花"商标无效行政案入选"新时代推动法治进程2022年度十大案件",为判断其他缺乏显著特征的标志提供了有效指导。审理"BIODERMA"商标申请驳回复审案,明确英文商标显著性的判断标准。审理"友联"商标无效宣告案,阐明违反诚信原则,未合理避让他人在先商标的商标不应予以注册。北京高院组建商标驳回复审案件、普通商标行政案件审判团队,推进案件集约化办理,商标驳回复审行政案件平均审理周期缩短至35天,切实实现简案快审、繁案精审。

（二）加大商标司法保护力度

不断强化商标使用对确定商标权保护范围的作用,积极引导权利人持续实际使用商标,发挥商标的识别功能,保护消费者合法权益。加强驰名商标、传统品牌和老字号司法保护,依法支持商标品牌建设。完善地理标志司法保护规则,遏制侵犯地理标志权利行为。最高人民法院审理"南庙"豆腐商标侵权案,依法保护其他经营者对注册商标中所含地名的正当使用。审理"一品石"商标侵权案，依法制止恶意取得商标并提起侵权诉讼的权利滥用行为。北京高院和北京知识产权法院积极为北京冬奥会和冬残奥会的奥运品牌保护工作提供支持，收到组委会发来的感谢信。四川高院依法处理"青花椒"商标维权案，维护商标使用秩序，保护诚信经营。浙江高院组织开展地理标志商标司法保护重点课题调研，助力地理标志司法保护水平提升。海南自由贸易港知识产权法院调研形成地理标志司法保护指南，探索知识产权保护与乡村振兴融合发展。北京西城法院走访辖区老字号企业，建立涉老字号知识产权案件挂账审理机制，促进"老字号"焕发"新活力"。

四、强化著作权审判，服务文化强国建设

人民法院充分发挥著作权审判对于优秀文化的引领和导向功能，加强著作权和相关权利保护，促进文化和科学事业发展与繁荣，服务社会主义文化强国建设。

（一）大力弘扬社会主义先进文化

立足司法审判职能，以社会主义核心价值观为引领，坚持弘扬社会主义先进文化，促进中华优秀传统文化创造性转化、创新性发展，激发全民族文化创新创造活力，增强实现中华民族伟大复兴的精神力量。依法审理涉及红色经典传承和英烈合法权益保护案件，大力弘扬社会主义核心价值观。加强遗传资源、传统文化、传统知识、民间文艺等著作权保护，促进非物质文化遗产的整理和利用。

高度重视网络直播、短视频、动漫游戏、文化创意等新领域著作权保护，打击盗版、抄袭行为，繁荣发展文化事业和文化产业。北京、天津、上海法院对盗播北京冬奥会、卡塔尔世界杯等行为及时作出禁令，促进优化数字文化市场环境。江苏宿迁中院分析研判当地图书盗版案件特点，向行政主管机关发送司法建议，有效遏制图书侵权盗版行为。广西钦州中院审结跨省制售盗版教材教辅著作权犯罪案，获评2022年全国青少年版权保护十大典型案件。北京互联网法院发布"版权链—天平链协同治理平台"2.0版本，实现数字版权确权、授权、交易、维权各环节全覆盖，推动版权要素市场健康有序发展。福建泉州德化法院构建陶瓷知识产权"1234"保护机制，推动破解证据保全、执法监管、社会认同、纠纷化解四大难题，获世界知识产权组织高度评价。

（二）提升新时代著作权司法水平

人民法院全面贯彻实施著作权法，保护著作权以及与著作权有关的权益。最高人民法院不断总结审判经验，组织地方法院共同开展调研，起草著作权司法解释，着力解决著作权审判领域法律适用疑难问题。依法提审并改判"大头儿子"美术作品著作权侵权案，厘清著作权归属认定规则，取得良好社会效果。办理侵害作品信息网络传播权管辖请示案，明确侵害信息网络传播权民事案件管辖问题及司法解释适用标准，有效指导著作权审判实践。北京高院就图片侵权案件许可使用费标准的确定形成答复，促进辖区图片侵权案件裁判尺度统一。湖北法院在著作权类型化案件审判中积极推广表格化裁判文书，大幅缩短审理周期。四川、重庆高院联合印发会议纪要，统一两地同类侵害信息网络传播权案件裁判标准。黑龙江高院与省版权局等九家单位就打击侵犯著作权违法犯罪会签通知文件，加强衔接配合，加大著作权刑事保护力度。北京知识产权法院统筹处理中文学术文献网络数据库企业间著作权侵权互诉系列案，一揽子促成全市 1000 余起案件调解，妥善化解潜在纠纷。

五、维护竞争法治环境，激发创新创造活力

人民法院持续加强反垄断和反不正当竞争司法，强化竞争政策基础地位，维护公平竞争的市场法治环境，优化营商环境，服务构建高水平社会主义市场经济体制。

（一）加强反垄断、反不正当竞争司法

2022 年，人民法院不断完善竞争领域法律适用规则，强化公平竞争司法审判，维护市场竞争法治秩序。最高人民法院出台《关于适用〈中华人民共和国反不正当竞争法〉若干问题的解释》，对反不正当竞争法"一般条款"、仿冒混淆、虚假宣传、商业诋毁、网络不正当竞争行为等问题作出细化规定，统一裁判标准，回应新领域新业态司法需求。研究起草新的反垄断民事诉讼司法解释，面向社会公开征求意见，推动健全完善反垄断案件裁判规则，明确垄断行为判断标准。召开人民法院加强反垄断和反不正当竞争司法新闻发布会，发布人民法院反垄断和反不正当竞争典型案例各 10 件，增强全社会尊重和保护公平竞争的法治意识，指导各级法院依法制裁垄断行为、维护公平竞争秩序。各级人民法院加强对平台经济、核心技

术、医药、通信等重点领域和关键环节的司法审判力度，严厉打击垄断协议，制止滥用市场支配地位等排除、限制竞争行为。完善涉互联网平台垄断行为认定标准，细化流量劫持、干扰等不正当竞争行为认定，依法规范和引导资本健康发展。最高人民法院审理"张百年"商标侵权及不正当竞争纠纷案和柏瑞润兴不正当竞争纠纷案，明确反不正当竞争纠纷案件中销售者责任。审理"幼儿园"横向垄断协议案和给排水公用企业滥用市场支配地位案，积极回应社会对事关百姓民生的市场竞争行为的关切，及时制止排除、限制竞争行为，切实保障人民群众从公平竞争中获益。

（二）依法促进数字经济健康发展

积极探索加强数字经济领域知识产权司法保护，为充分发挥数据要素作用、提高数据要素治理效能提供有力司法服务和保障，促进数字经济实现高质量发展。加强数据云存储、数据开源、数据确权、数据交易、数据服务、数据市场不正当竞争等案件审理，切实维护数据安全。开展数据权益知识产权司法保护调研和数字经济时代公平竞争与知识产权司法保护调研，指导地方法院探索数字经济审判模式，促进数字经济创新成果的司法保护。最高人民法院审理"爬虫平台数据信息"技术秘密侵权案，明确平台数据信息可以作为技术秘密保护客体，强化对平台经营者通过合法经营形成的具有竞争优势和竞争价值的数据权益保护。江西高院制定知识产权审判服务保障数字经济发展的意见，提出13项服务与保障举措。广东深圳中院出台加强数字经济知识产权司法保护的实施意见，助力深圳数字经济高质量发展。北京知识产权法院完成"数字经济下新业态、新模式竞争行为司法规制研究"等课题，妥善审结多起数据侵权案，不断探索适用反不正当竞争法保护数据的裁判规则。

六、深入推进司法改革，提升整体保护效能

人民法院深入推进知识产权审判领域改革创新，不断完善知识产权专门化审判体系，健全知识产权诉讼制度，深化知识产权审判"三合一"改革，统一法律适用标准，加强纠纷多元化解，强化行政执法和司法衔接，促进知识产权司法保护效能全面提升。

（一）推进审判体系现代化提升司法能力

以最高人民法院知识产权审判部门为牵引、4个知识产权法院为示范、27个地方中级人民法院知识产权法庭为重点、地方各级人民法院知识产权审判庭为支撑的专业化审判格局进一步完善。最高人民法院制定《关于第一审知识产权民事、行政案件管辖的若干规定》，配套发布《关于印发基层人民法院管辖第一审知识产权民事、行政案件标准的通知》和《关于涉及发明专利等知识产权合同纠纷案件上诉管辖问题的通知》，健全管辖科学的司法保护体制，合理定位四级法院审判职能，优化审判资源配置，全国具有知识产权民事案件管辖权的基层法院包括互联网法院已经达558家。最高人民法院不断完善国家层面知识产权案件上诉审理机制，优化知识产权申请再审案件办理流程，加强监督指导，确保法律正确统一适用。地方各级人民法院调配审判资源、依法适用案件提级管辖等机制，推动知识产权案件的高效审理和当事人权益的充分保障。

最高人民法院加大指导力度，推进全国25个高级法院、236个中级法院和275个基层法院开展知识产权民事、行政和刑事案件"三合一"审判机制改革，十地法院已实现辖区内知识产权案件"三合一"审理机制全覆盖。积极推动相关规范性文件研究制定，会同最高人民检察院起草《关于办理侵犯知识产权刑事案件适用法律若干问题的解释（征求意见稿）》并向社会公开征求意见。黑龙江高院协调有关部门为省内受理知识产权案件的中级、基层法院审判庭加挂"知识产权审判庭"牌子，印发实施方案，指导"三合一"工作落地见效。安徽、浙江、河南、青海等地高院与省检察院、省公安厅联合出台完善知识产权刑事案件管辖的指导文件，明确程序衔接，健全协调机制，全面落实"三合一"改革目标。

持续完善多元化技术事实查明机制，加强"全国法院技术调查人才库"建设，超500名技术调查专家入库，全国范围按需调派和人才共享机制不断深化，有效缓解技术类案件事实查明难题。广西、西藏等地高院出台技术调查官参与知识产权诉讼案件办理的相关规定，结合地方实际完善制度机制。南京、苏州知识产权法庭充分发挥技术调查官作用，参与751件技术类案件事实调查，参与勘验、保全66次，庭审、听证490次，出具技术调查报告388份。

人民法院积极探索健全完善知识产权司法保护规则。最高人民法院出台《关于加强中医药知识产权司法保护的意见》，促进中医药传承创新发展。针对知识产权诉讼特点，推动知识产权诉讼特别程序法研究制定。开展知识产权恶意诉讼规制、惩罚性赔偿精准适用等领域的专项调研，着力遏制滥用权利，加强权利人保护。上海高院印发知识产权小额诉讼案件办理意见，推动知识产权案件繁简分流、小额诉讼程序优化调整。北京、山东、广东、新疆、内蒙古等地高院及中院，起草或出台惩罚性赔偿的适用指引，发布典型案例，促进惩罚性赔偿制度依法严格准确落实。

（二）参与构建知识产权大保护格局

持续加强司法审判与行政执法衔接协作，促进行政执法标准与司法裁判标准统一。最高人民法院会同最高人民检察院、农业农村部、商务部、文化和旅游部、国家市场监督管理总局、国家知识产权局、国家中医药管理局等单位，完善协同配合机制，推进业务交流、数据交换和信息共享。与国家知识产权局、最高人民检察院等部门印发《关于加强知识产权鉴定工作衔接的意见》，深化知识产权管理执法部门与司法机关在知识产权鉴定工作中的合作。与国家知识产权局联合印发《关于强化知识产权协同保护的意见》，健全知识产权行政保护与司法保护衔接的13项具体举措。陕西高院牵头与13家省级机关及院校单位成立秦创原知识产权司法保护中心，建立联席会议制度，搭建合作平台。广州知识产权法院、上海知识产权法院与国家知识产权局开展协作，探索专利行政确权和法院侵权纠纷审理同步进行，有效缩短专利侵权案件审理周期，提升保护效果。

积极推进知识产权纠纷多元化解机制建设，深化落实"总对总"在线诉调对接工作机制，完善行政调解协议司法确认制度，促进形成知识产权保护合力。全国30个地区实现知识产权调解组织全覆盖，入驻调解组织、调解员持续增长，人民法院委派诉前调解纠纷9万余件，调解成功率超过80%，有效化解知识产权纠纷。最高人民法院加强与国家版权局、中国作家协会、中国文联等单位的沟通，推动建立版权保护领域"总对总"在线诉调对接机制。河北高院与省市场监管局联合签署《知识产权纠纷行政调解协议司法确认工作合作备忘录》，推动5件专利纠纷通过行政调解协议司法确认机制化解。山东法院全年办理知识产权纠纷行政调解协议司法确认案件146件。辽宁高院联合省知识产权局印发《关于建立知识产权纠纷在线诉调对接机制的通知》，成立11个调解组织，110名调解员入驻，2834件知识产权纠纷调解成功，成功率达96.29%。黑龙江高院配合省司法厅组建设立知识产权仲裁院，下发《关于依法妥善办理仲裁保全案件的通知》，推动诉讼与仲裁、调解衔接，强化协同治理。

推动构建区域知识产权保护机制，加强知识产权诚信体系建设，扩大知识产权司法保护法治宣传。最高人民法院持续指导相关法院，积极服务京津冀协同发展、长江经济带发展、长三角一体化发展、粤港澳大湾区建设、东北全面振兴、海南自由贸易港建设、成渝地区双城经济圈建设等，助推区域协同创新。湖南、湖北、江西高院推动"长江中游城市群"审判工作协作机制，指导岳阳、咸宁、九江等地中院和有关市场监管部门签订跨域知识产权保护协议，探索解决跨区域、规模化、群体性知识产权侵权新问题。四川、重庆高院联合举办2022川渝知识产权保护研讨会，强化两地知识产权一体化保护。北京知识产权法院与天津市三中院、雄安新区中院签署《关于加强知识产权司法保护合作框架协议》，推动人才培养、协同审判、经验分享等方面合作。海南自由贸易港知识产权法院向海南省市场监管局、省知识产权局发出司法建议,将9起侵犯知识产权刑事案件的12人列入知识产权严重违法失信主体名单,向社会公示。辽宁大连中院向当地市场监管局发出司法建议,对4名主体故意侵害知识产权的行为予以公示。天津滨海新区法院出台规定,将知识产权案件被执行人不履行义务的信息向市场监管部门、金融机构及行业协会等通报。知识产权宣传周期间,最高人民法院召开新闻发布会,组织系列活动,全方位、多视角、深层次展示人民法院知识产权司法保护成果。吉林、甘肃、青海、宁夏、新疆生产建设兵团等地法院精心组织发布典型案例,开展公开庭审、公开执行等活动,促进增强全社会尊重和保护知识产权意识。

七、坚持依法平等保护,促进国际交流合作

深入推进国际知识产权诉讼优选地建设,妥善审理与国际贸易有关的重大知识产权纠纷,营造公开透明的法治环境和平等竞争的市场环境,积极服务高水平对外开放。2022年,全国法院审结涉外知识产权一审案件近9000件。最高人民法院审理马诺娄·布拉尼克与国家知识产权局等商标权无效行政纠纷案,平等保护外国当事人在先权利,西班牙驻中国大使馆发函表示感谢。江苏法院新收涉外知识产权案件527件,审结涉外国知名品牌商标侵权及不正当竞争纠纷案,依法适用惩罚性赔偿,全额支持外方权利人5000万元赔偿请求。广东法院妥善化解系列涉外标准必要专利纠纷,促成当事方达成全球一揽子和解。福建厦门思明法院与一带一路国际商事调解

中心共同设立海丝中央法务区知识产权专业调解室，拓宽涉外知识产权纠纷调解途径。

坚持人类命运共同体理念，积极参与世界知识产权组织框架下的全球知识产权治理，深化同其他国家和地区知识产权司法合作，推动完善相关国际规则和标准。参加第3届中国—东盟大法官论坛、中国—新加坡最高法院联合工作组第四次会议，与欧盟举办知识产权专门诉讼程序研讨会，参加2022年世界知识产权组织法官论坛、替代性争议解决机制平行论坛、执法咨询委员会第十五届会议，参加商务部举办的中俄知识产权工作组第13次会议等会议，与香港特别行政区政府律政司共同举办内地与香港知识产权纠纷案件法律适用与司法合作研讨会，参与世界知识产权组织《国际专利案件管理司法指南》中国专章的编写和远程教育中文项目高级课程授课。福建高院与世界知识产权组织仲裁与调解中心签署《加强知识产权领域替代性争议解决交流与合作协议》，制定配套对接工作办法。

八、发挥党建引领作用，锻造一流审判队伍

人民法院始终坚持以党的政治建设为统领，坚决筑牢政治忠诚，公正廉洁司法，努力锻造一支政治坚定、顾全大局、精通法律、熟悉技术、具有国际视野的知识产权审判队伍。

党的二十大是在全党全国各族人民迈上全面建设社会主义现代化国家新征程、向第二个百年奋斗目标进军的关键时刻召开的一次十分重要的大会，擘画了以中国式现代化全面推进中华民族伟大

复兴的宏伟蓝图，专门就加强知识产权法治保障作出部署。人民法院牢牢坚持党对知识产权司法工作的绝对领导，坚定拥护"两个确立"、坚决做到"两个维护"，全面学习、全面把握、全面落实党的二十大精神，坚持不懈用习近平新时代中国特色社会主义思想凝心铸魂，坚持用习近平法治思想指导新时代知识产权司法，深入开展"两个确立"主题教育，巩固深化党史学习教育和政法队伍教育整顿成果，不断推动人民法院知识产权司法审判工作实现高质量发展。

严格执行防止干预司法"三个规定"、新时代政法干警"十个严禁"等铁规禁令，落实近亲属"禁业清单"，规范离任从业行为，全面准确落实司法责任制、规范司法权力运行、完善知识产权领域审判权力运行和制约监督机制，确保公正廉洁司法。不断加大教育培训力度，提升干警政治理论水平和业务能力素质，增强斗争精神和斗争本领。最高人民法院就新制定的知识产权类司法解释和司法政策性文件召开新闻通报会，发布理解与适用文章，指导地方各级人民法院准确适用。组织力量完成《中国民法典适用大全》知识产权与竞争卷内容的编写，开展裁判要旨梳理提炼工作，进一步有效指导审判实践。四川、重庆高院与两地省（市）检察院共同举办知识产权司法保护业务培训班，指导成都中院与重庆一中院共同承办知识产权法官论坛。云南高院与省市场监管局联合举办知识产权行政执法与司法保护培训班，提升知识产权法官眼界视野。辽宁丹东中院结合边境口岸城市特点，联合海关开展培训，促进知识产权审判工作人员了解国际品牌保护。

结束语

　　2023年是全面贯彻落实党的二十大精神的开局之年，人民法院知识产权审判将坚持以习近平新时代中国特色社会主义思想为指导，全面贯彻落实党的二十大和二十届一中、二中全会精神，深入贯彻习近平法治思想，深刻领悟"两个确立"的决定性意义，增强"四个意识"、坚定"四个自信"、做到"两个维护"，牢牢坚持党的绝对领导，坚定不移走中国特色社会主义法治道路。紧紧围绕"努力让人民群众在每一个司法案件中感受到公平正义"目标，坚持讲政治顾大局、促公正提效率、重自律强队伍，始终做到司法为民、公正司法。进一步"加强知识产权法治保障，有力支持全面创新"，营造开放、公平、公正、非歧视的科技发展环境，以及市场化、法治化、国际化一流营商环境，为全面建设社会主义现代化国家开好局起好步贡献力量。

附件：

2022年全国法院新收知识产权案件类型与数量图

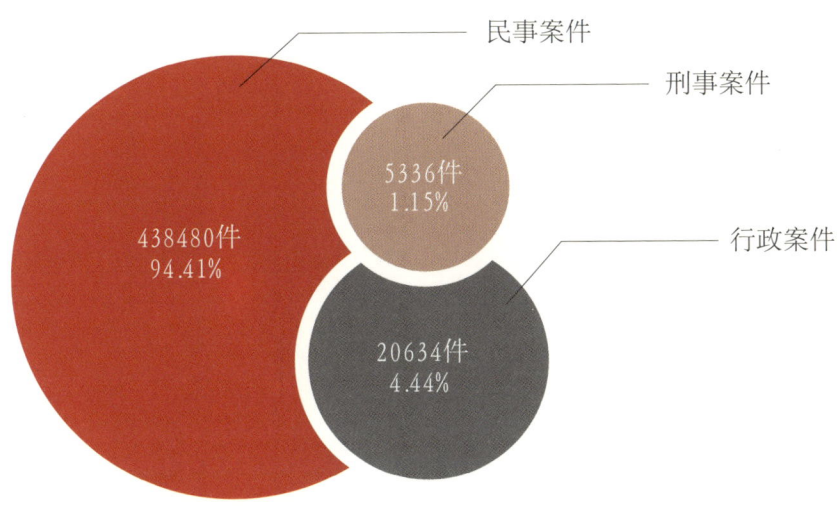

图1 2022年全国地方人民法院新收知识产权一审案件类型与数量

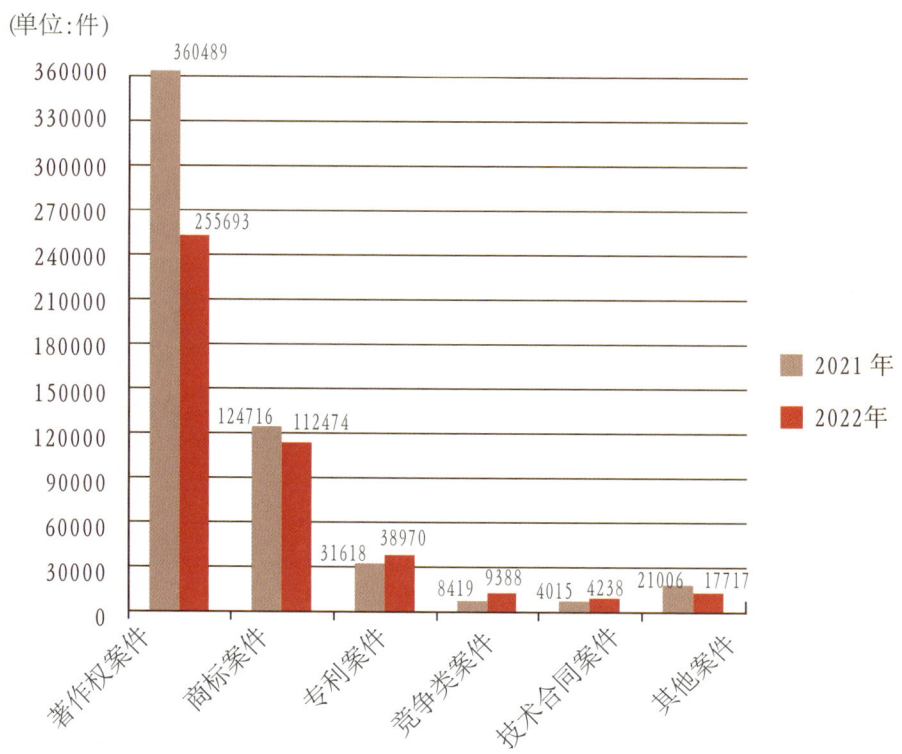

图 2　2022年与2021年全国地方人民法院新收知识产权民事一审案件数量对比

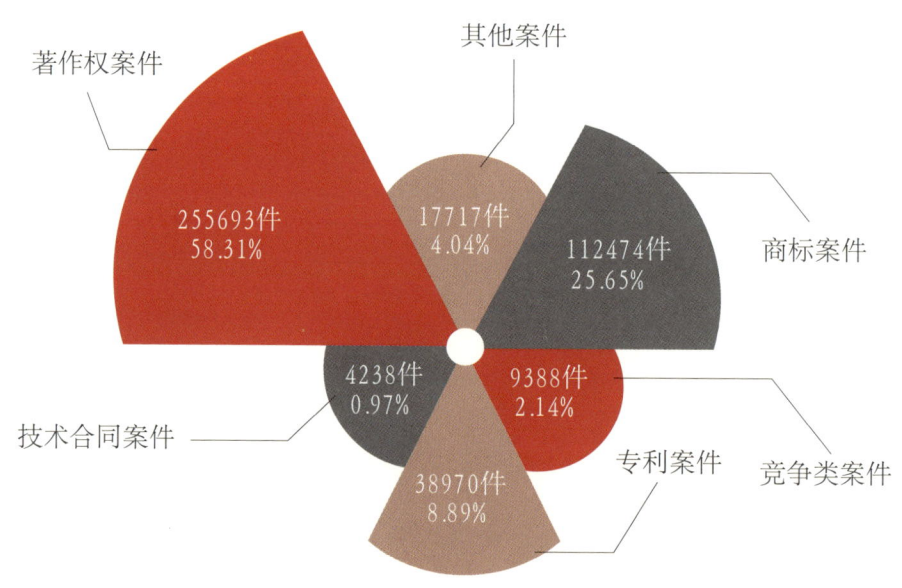

图 3　2022年全国地方人民法院新收知识产权民事一审案件类型与数量

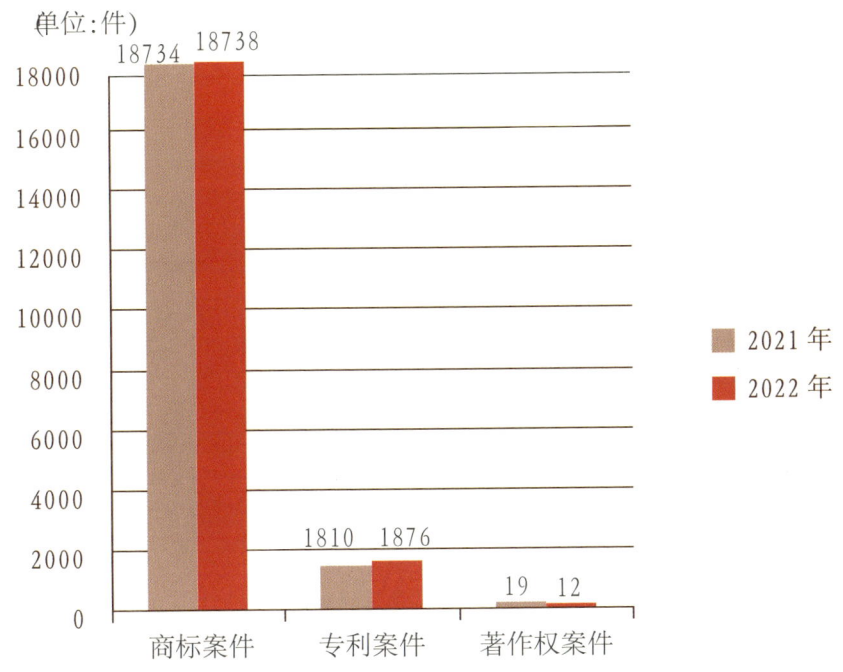

图4 2022年与2021年全国地方人民法院新收知识产权行政一审案件数量对比

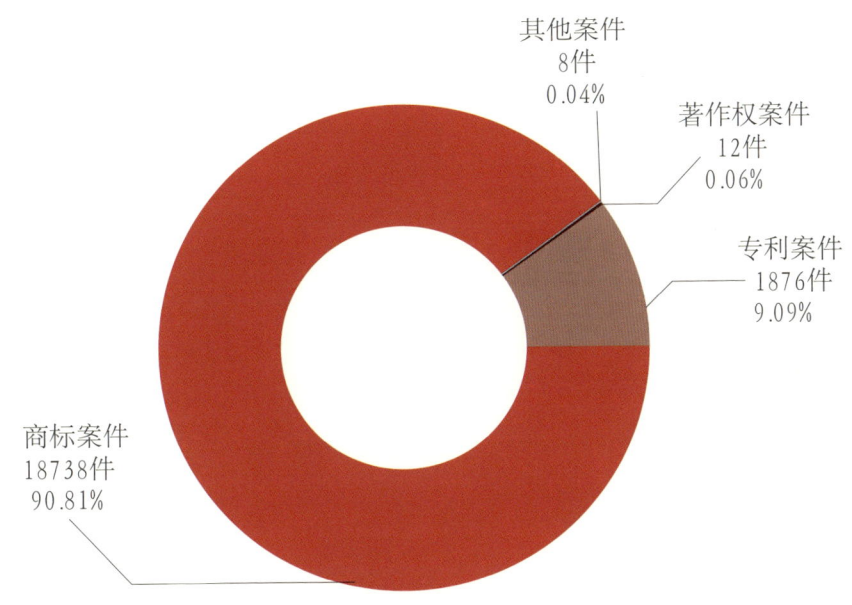

图5 2022年全国地方人民法院新收知识产权行政一审案件类型与数量

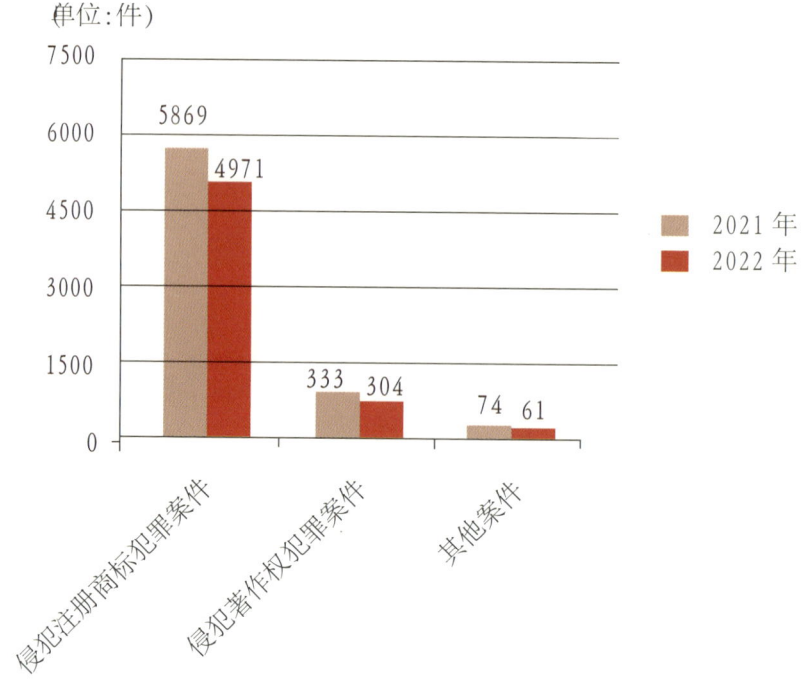

图6 2022年与2021年全国地方人民法院新收知识产权刑事一审案件数量对比

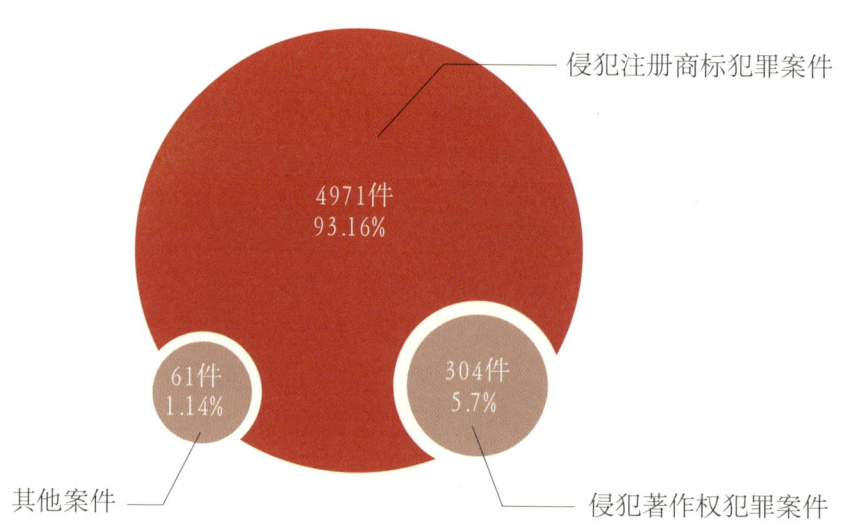

图7 2022年全国地方人民法院新收知识产权刑事一审案件类型与数量

Judicial Protection of Intellectual Property Rights in Chinese Courts (2022)

Introduction

In the Report to the 20th National Congress of the Communist Party of China, it was emphasized that pursuing high-quality development is one of the essential requirements of the Chinese path to modernization and innovation will remain at the core of China's modernization drive, and special deployment was made to strengthen the legal protection of intellectual property rights. In 2022, Chinese courts adhered to Xi Jinping Thought on Socialism with Chinese Characteristics for a New Era, put the guiding principles from the 20th National Congress into action, and fully implemented Xi Jinping Thought on the Rule of Law, while keeping in mind the top priorities of the country. In order to make the people feel justice has been served in each and every judicial case, Chinese courts enhanced the sense of responsibility and mission in improving the trial of intellectual property (hereinafter "IP") cases in the new era and continued to improve judicial protection of IP rights.

I. Fully Utilizing Trial Functions to Support Innovation-Driven Development

In 2022, Chinese courts focused on bolstering their trial functions, while trying various IP cases fairly and efficiently in accordance with the law. The courts newly accepted 526,165 IP cases of first instance, second instance, and remanded for retrial, and concluded 543,379 cases (including carried over cases, ditto hereinafter), a year-on-year decrease of 18.17% and 9.67%, respectively.

In 2022, local people's courts at all levels newly accepted 438,480 civil IP cases of first instance and concluded 457,805, a year-on-year decrease of 20.31% and 11.25%, respectively. In these newly accepted cases, the number of patent cases increased by 23.25% to 38,970 from the previous year, trademark cases dropped by 9.82% to 112,474 year on year, copyright cases decreased by 29.07% to 255,693, technology contract cases grew by 5.55% to 4,238, competition cases increased by 11.51% to 9,388, and other cases of civil IP disputes fell by 15.66% to 17,717 year on year. In 2022, local courts newly accepted 46,524 civil IP cases of second instance, down 5.22% year on year, and concluded 46,563, up 2.41% on a year-on-year basis. The Supreme People's Court newly accepted 3,786 civil IP cases and concluded 3,073, a year-on-year drop of 10.77% and 13.61%, respectively.

In 2022, local courts newly accepted 20,634 administrative IP cases of first instance and concluded 17,630, a year-on-year increase of 0.35% and decrease of 8.85%, respectively. Among those newly accepted cases, the number of patent cases increased by 3.65% to 1,876, trademark cases grew by 4 to 18,738, and copyright cases fell by 7 to 12. In addition, local courts newly accepted 5,897 administrative IP cases of second instance and concluded 7,285, down 28.22% and 1.79% respectively compared to 2021. Of those cases, 5,518 were sustained, 1,650 were reversed, 3 were remanded for retrial, 78 were withdrawn, 10 were dismissed, and 26 were resolved in other means. The Supreme People's Court newly accepted 1,456 administrative IP cases, a drop of 48.95% compared to 2021, and concluded 1,542, down 38% year on year.

Local courts newly accepted 5,336 criminal IP infringement cases of first instance and concluded 5,456, down 14.98% and 9.76% respectively. In particular, 4,971 trademark infringement criminal cases were newly accepted, and 5,099 were concluded, a year-on-year drop of 15.3% and 9.86%, respectively; 304 copyright infringement criminal cases were newly accepted, and 302 were concluded, down 8.71% and 7.93%, respectively. Other criminal cases newly accepted reached 61, and 55 were concluded, down 13 and 6 respectively compared to the figures of 2021. Local courts newly accepted 979 criminal IP cases of second instance and concluded 977, a decrease of 6.76% and 2.01% compared to 2021, respectively.

In 2022, IP cases accepted by Chinese courts are mainly characterized by the following features:

The number of technology-related cases continued to increase, the demand for IP rights protection in central and western China was high, and the importance of IPR judicial services to high-quality development was emphasized further. In 2022, the IP Court of the Supreme People's Court continued to accept a significant number of new civil non-procedural cases in second instance involving technical IP rights. Significantly more cases of first instance involving patent and technology contracts were accepted by local people's courts at all levels. Courts in Jiangsu province newly accepted 1,817 cases of disputes over ownership and infringement of technical IP rights, a 17.61% increase from the previous year. Year-on-year, the number of new IPR cases received by the courts in Shanxi province and Hainan province rose by

22.21% and 72.58%, respectively. In Hebei province, the number of IP cases newly accepted and concluded by local courts increased by 45.94% and 106.01% year on year, respectively. The number of new civil IPR cases received in courts of Liaoning province increased by 61% annually. The number of new civil IPR cases of first instance accepted by courts in Jiangxi province increased by 22% compared to 2021. In addition, the number of cases accepted by the courts in Hunan province, Heilongjiang province, and the Xinjiang Production and Construction Corps (hereinafter referred to as "XPCC") also continued to grow steadily.

The Internet online trial mechanism for IP cases continued to see innovations, the development of smart court architecture was fostered, and the mechanism for convenience and benefit of the judiciary was improved. Online trial platforms were leveraged by local courts to facilitate online court hearings, services, and other legal processes of IP cases, which shortened the duration of litigation and reduced litigation costs. For instance, courts in Shanghai accepted 38,505 IP cases online, with over 20,000 online court hearings and meetings and more than 170,000 electronic services. Courts in Henan province recorded an online filing rate of over 90%, with 16,023 IP first instance cases were filed online. In Qinghai, the online filing rate for IP cases reached 62.7%, with 898 electronic services were conducted via the service platform. In

Guangxi, the Intermediate People's Court of Guigang utilized digital technology to have approximately 70% of all accepted IP cases filed online annually. The Qingdao Intellectual Property Court developed an online asynchronous evidence cross-examination system, which enabled relevant parties to upload electronic evidence online and complete cross-examination, thereby streamlining pre-trial procedures.

The substantive resolution of disputes by Chinese courts continued to be strengthened, and the protection of the rights and interests of rights holders became more comprehensive, which increased public satisfaction with the judicial protection of IP rights. Local Chinese courts mediated and resolved 44,155 civil IP cases of first instance, a mediation and resolution rate of 9.64%, up 0.78% compared to 2021. Additionally, 2,894 civil IP cases of second instance were mediated and resolved at a rate of 6.22%, an increase of 0.57% from the previous year. Notably, the rates of mediation and withdrawal of IP cases recorded by courts in Tianjin, as well as Hebei, Guangdong, and Heilongjiang provinces were particularly high, reaching 75.51%, 73.48%, 52.94%, and 66.6%, respectively. The high rates of withdrawal reflect the effective reduction of the burden on litigants and the complete maintenance of social stability and harmony. Courts in Jiangsu province heard 97 IP cases in which punitive damages were applied, up 21.25% year on year. The Primary

People's Court of Pudong New Area of Shanghai applied punitive damages in 25 cases. A total of 169 million yuan was awarded as punitive damages for 29 IP cases heard by the Intermediate People's Court of Shenzhen. Local courts in Hunan province conducted a special judicial campaign and concluded 3,796 cases involving IP rights, with 60.4315 million yuan awarded. In Guangdong province, less than 20% of civil IP cases accepted by local courts resulted in forced enforcement, with a 98% enforcement and closing rate. In response to IP infringement in critical areas influencing people's livelihoods, such as food and drug production, courts in Jiangsu province issued nearly one hundred orders prohibiting the relevant entities from engaging in the specified industry. According to the relevant applications, the Intermediate People's Court of Guiyang in Guizhou province heard 25 IP preservation cases and froze properties worth 40.1 million yuan. The cost of IP infringement increased dramatically, and rights holders were effectively compensated for their losses.

More cases were accepted by courts at lower levels. The quality and effectiveness of IP case trials have been improved as a result of jurisdiction diversity of intermediate and high courts. In Jiangsu province, primary people's courts heard 65.25% of all IP cases in the province, an increase of 10.52% year on year. Meanwhile, the proportion of cases heard by intermediate and high courts dropped to 31.56% and 3.19%, respectively. Similarly, in Chongqing, the number of IP cases newly accepted by primary people's courts accounted for 75.2% of all IP cases in the city, up 28.1% compared to 2021; the proportion of cases heard by intermediate and high courts, in contrast, decreased by 29.9% to 21.3% and increased by 1.8% to 3.5%, respectively. This demonstrates the gradual formation of a "pyramid" pattern with respect to the trial of IP cases. Of the first-instance civil IP cases concluded by local courts, 320 cases were concluded under the elevated jurisdiction of higher courts, more than three times of those in 2021. 63 civil IP cases were submitted to a higher-level court in Jiangxi province, and 15 such cases were submitted to a higher court in Guangdong province due to their novelty, complexity, or guiding significance in law application, thus effectively promoting the uniformity of judicial rules.

II. Encouraging and Assuring Scientific and Technological Innovation to Promote Self-reliance and Strength

Speeding up efforts to achieve greater self-reliance and strength in science and technology is the path China must take to advance high-quality development. Chinese courts maximized the role of IP trials in fostering and safeguarding scientific and technological innovation. Chinese courts provided high-quality judicial services to support basic research, protected original and pioneering scientific and technological advances, and eliminated obstacles that impeded high-quality development.

1. Chinese Courts Continued to Promote the Unification of Judicial Standards in Technology-Related Cases

Concentrating on bolstering IP protection, Chinese courts conducted a more stringent examination of the legitimacy of administrative acts pertaining to patent granting and rights reexamination and promoted the application of unified administrative and judicial standards, thereby enhancing the quality of patent granting and rights reexamination. In 2022, Chinese courts maximized their responsibilities in rule-setting and value guidance for protecting achievements of scientific and technological innovation, summarized and proposed new judicial protection rules, and encouraged the continuous innovation and upgrading of technologies and industries. The Supreme People's Court reasonably defined the trial functions of courts at four levels and specified that cases involving ownership and infringement disputes related to invention patents, utility model patents, new plant varieties, integrated circuit layout designs, trade secrets, and computer software should be centrally adjudicated by the intellectual property courts, intermediate people's courts of provincial capitals, and intermediate people's courts designated by the Supreme People's Court. This effectively promoted the nationwide application of consistent judicial standards in technology-related cases and improved judicial protection of significant scientific and technological innovations. The Supreme People's Court released the Top 10 Intellectual Property Cases and 50 Typical Intellectual Property Cases in 2021, including 11 technology-related cases involving infringement of technology secrets, plant variety rights, and invention patents, which provided useful guidance for trial practices. In addition, the Supreme People's Court conducted research on the implementation of judicial interpretations such as *Provisions on Several Issues concerning the Application of Law in the Trial of Civil Cases Involving Patent Disputes Related to Drugs Applied for Registration* in order to quickly summarize the trial experience. In the trial of the patent right ownership dispute over the "dust removal device and system for gasification furnaces", the Supreme People's Court defined the right basis for the source party and the technology improvement party. In the trial of the administrative dispute over the invalidity of the patent rights between Qilu Pharmaceutical and Sihuan Pharmaceutical, the judicial standards for the creativity of drug patents and adequate disclosure in specifications were clarified. In the trial of the infringement dispute over the utility model patent rights of the "integral geocell", it was determined whether the defense concerning a legitimate source complied with reasonable diligence requirements.

2. Chinese Courts Committed to Facilitate and Protect Basic Research and Original Innovation

Based on the requirement that the frontier science and technology in the world should be integrated with the major national strategic needs, economic and social development goals and the livelihoods and wellbeing of the people, Chinese courts intensified IP protection in key areas, core technologies, and emerging industries. Meanwhile, the courts worked to ensure the legitimate rights and interests of innovators and provided judicial services to achieve breakthroughs in core technologies. The Supreme People's Court implemented the arrangements of the Central Committee of the Communist Party of China on the revitalization of the seed industry and issued the *Guiding Opinions on Protecting the Intellectual Property Rights of the Seed Industry, Combating Infringement of Counterfeit and Inferior Goods, and Creating a Good Environment for the Revitalization of the Seed Industry* jointly with the Ministry of Agriculture and Rural Affairs and other departments. In addition, the Supreme People's Court released the second group of model cases from Chinese courts regarding judicial protection of IP rights in the seed industry, supported the establishment of the Base of Chinese Courts for the IP Protection in Germplasm Resource Research (Hainan), and held the Seminar of Judicial Protection for IP Rights in Germplasm Resource for the first time in the name of the Base. The case of the "Jinjing 818" rice plant variety infringement was selected as one of the "Top Ten Cases of Promoting the Progress of the Rule of Law in the New Era in 2021". The Supreme People's Court concluded China's first drug patent linkage lawsuit, which was nominated as one of the "Top Ten Cases of Promoting the Progress of the Rule of Law in the New Era in 2022" and accelerated to shape and improve the drug patent linkage system. In the two related cases of patent and technology secret infringement involving "melamine", the defendants were ordered to compensate the rights holders for a total of 218 million yuan in economic losses with several and joint liabilities, which reflects the judicial goal of vigorously protecting technological innovation. During the trial of the technology secret infringement case of "oil and gas microorganism exploration", the Supreme People's Court delivered a strong signal to improve the protection of technology secrets. The High People's Court of Jiangsu Province, along with the competent provincial departments, signed a memorandum of understanding on "Building Strong Industrial Chains via IP Protection and Developing an Independent and Self-controlled Modern Industrial System", which established a working mechanism to develop the key industrial chains. Suzhou Intellectual

Property Tribunal facilitated a package settlement between the parties in an invention patent infringement dispute involving a US corporation, effectively protecting the legitimate rights and interests of innovators. Hefei Intellectual Property Tribunal met with administrative and law enforcement agencies as well as companies based in Anhui province, to solicit and respond to commercial innovators for rights protection.

III. Increasing Judicial Protection of Trademarks to Enable the Growth of Successful Brands

Chinese courts continued to strengthen the judicial protection of trademark rights, improved the trial quality of administrative cases on trademark registration and review, as well as civil cases on trademarks, and upheld the order of trademark application, registration, and use. They directed rights holders to register trademarks in compliance with the law, regulated the use of trademarks, and upheld the rule of law on the market, thereby encouraging the growth of successful Chinese brands in the new era.

1. Chinese Courts Improved the Quality of Trademark Registration and Review

In order to improve the trial quality of administrative cases involving trademark registration and review, steps have been taken to crack down on malicious trademark registration for the non-purpose of use. The boundaries and protective scopes of trademark rights were reasonably defined, and normalized, standardized procedures for trademark application and registration were promoted. The Supreme People's Court and China National Intellectual Property Administration co-hosted a symposium to solicit opinions from courts across the country and provide sound suggestions and references for legislation work such as the revision of trademark laws and the legislation of geographical indications, as well as promote the continuous improvement of the legal system for trademark regulations, which further improved the rules for trademark registration and review. The administrative case concluded by the Supreme People's Court regarding the invalidation of the trademark "Chen Mahua" was selected as one of the "Top Ten Cases of Promoting the Progress of the Rule of Law in the New Era in 2022", which provided effective guidance for rulings of trademarks lacking distinctive features. The criteria for determining the distinctiveness of English trademarks were clarified during the retrial of the denied "BIODERMA" trademark application. In the case regarding the invalidation of the "Youlian" trademark, it was stated that trademarks violated the principle of good faith and failed to reasonably avoid prior registered trademarks should not be registered. Beijing High People's Court established two distinct teams to try administrative trademark rejection review cases and administrative cases proceeding involving regular trademarks. This facilitated the intensive case management and reduced the average review time for administrative trademark rejection review cases to 35 days, making it possible to "quickly try simple cases, and scrutinize complicated cases".

2. Chinese Courts Strengthened the Judicial Protection of Trademarks

People's courts continued to strengthen the role of trademark usage in determining the scope of trademark right protection and encouraged trademark owners to use trademarks in practice continuously to give full play to the identification function of trademarks, while protecting the legitimate rights and interests of consumers. In accordance with the law, the judicial protection of well-known trademarks, traditional brands, and time-honored brands was strengthened, and the development of brands was encouraged. The rules and regulations for protecting geographical indications were improved, and infringement on geographical indication rights were curtailed. During the trademark infringement case trial of the "Nanmiao" tofu, the Supreme People's Court protected the legitimate use of the geographical name in the registered trademark by other operators. In the "Yipinshi" trademark infringement case trial, the abusive use of rights by maliciously obtaining trademarks and initiating infringement lawsuits was halted in accordance with the law. The organizing committee of the Beijing Winter Olympics and Paralympic Winter Olympics sent a letter of appreciation to Beijing High People's Court and the Beijing Intellectual Property Court for supporting the protection of Olympic brands. The High People's Court of Sichuan Province heard the "Qinhuajiao(green pepper)" trademark infringement case in accordance with the law, which maintained the order of trademark usage, and safeguarded ethical business practices. To enhance judicial protection of geographical indications, the High People's Court of Zhejiang Province launched a major research project initiative on the judicial protection of trademarks with geographical indications. The Intellectual Property Court of Hainan Free Trade Port conducted research to develop a guide for judicial protection of geographical indications, exploring the integration of IP protection and rural revitalization. Xicheng Primary People's Court, Beijing visited time-honored brands within its jurisdiction and established a IP cases trial supervisory mechanism to promote time-honored brands rejuvenation.

IV. Strengthening Copyright Trials to Contribute to the Building of a Country with a Strong Culture

People's courts fully leveraged the guiding role of copyright trials in promoting outstanding culture, strengthened protection of copyright and related rights, promoted the development of culture and science, and contributed to the building of a socialist country with a strong culture.

1. Chinese Courts Vigorously Promoted Advanced Socialist Culture

Chinese courts continued to be dedicated to promoting advanced socialist culture based on their functions in judicial trials. They also facilitated the creative transformation and innovative development of fine traditional Chinese culture, and sparked the creative vitality for cultural innovation and creation, thereby bolstering the cultural-ethical driving force necessary to realize the great rejuvenation of the Chinese nation. Chinese courts heard cases involving the inheritance of classic Chinese revolutionary works and the protection of the legitimate rights and interests of heroes, heroines and martyrs according to the law, while vigorously promoting the core socialist values. Copyright protection for genetic resources, traditional culture, traditional knowledge, and folk art was intensified to promote the consolidation and utilization of intangible cultural heritage. Chinese courts prioritized copyright protection in new areas such as live streaming, short videos, animation and games, and cultural creativity, clamping down on piracy and plagiarism while promoting the prosperous development of cultural undertakings and industries. To improve the market environment for digital culture, courts in Beijing, Tianjin, and Shanghai issued injunctions against behaviors such as the piracy of broadcasting the Beijing Winter Olympics and the Qatar World Cup. The Intermediate People's Court of Suqian, Jiangsu Province analyzed the characteristics of local book piracy cases and submitted judicial recommendations to the administrative authority, which effectively reduced book infringements and piracies. The Intermediate People's Court of Qinzhou, Guangxi Zhuang Autonomous Region concluded a cross-provincial copyright infringement crime case involving the sale of pirated textbooks and reference books , which was selected as one of the "Top Ten Typical Cases of Youth Copyright Protection in 2022". Beijing Internet Court released version 2.0 of the Tianping Blockchain-Copyright Chain co-governance platform, which achieved full coverage of digital copyright rights confirmation, authorization, transaction, and protection, thereby promoting the development of the copyright market in a healthy and orderly manner. Dehua Primary People's Court, Quanzhou, Fujian Province established a "1-2-3-4" protection mechanism targeting ceramic IP rights to address 4 main challenges: evidence preservation, law enforcement & supervision, social recognition, and dispute resolution, which was formally acknowledged by the World Intellectual Property Organization (WIPO).

2. Chinese Courts Enhanced Judicial Protection of Copyright in the New Era

People's courts fully implemented the Copyright Law to protect copyright and related rights. The Supreme People's Court continued to summarize judicial experiences and conducted researches jointly with local courts, and drafted judicial interpretations of the Copyright Law to solve challenging legal issues in the field of copyright trials. The Supreme People's Court heard and reversed the judgment on the copyright infringement case of the "Big-Headed Kid" artwork, which clarified the rules for determining copyright ownership and achieved positive social effects. In a case involving the jurisdiction query for the infringement of the right to disseminate works over the Internet, the Supreme People's Court specified the jurisdiction of civil cases involving such infringement and the judicial interpretation application standards, providing sound guidance for copyright trial practices. Beijing High People's Court provided a reply on determining the royalty standards for image infringement cases, which promoted the adoption of consistent judicial standards concerning similar cases in its jurisdiction. In Hubei province, local courts promoted the use of standardized table judgment in copyright cases, which significantly shortened the trial period. Sichuan High People's Court and Chongqing High People's Court jointly issued minutes to unify the judicial standards concerning infringement of the right to disseminate information over the Internet in their jurisdictions. Heilongjiang High People's Court, along with 9 other government departments including Heilongjiang Provincial Copyright Administration, jointly signed a notice to crack down on violations of the Copyright Law to strengthen criminal protection of copyright. Beijing Intellectual Property Court made well-coordinated efforts and mediated a series of lawsuits between companies regarding copyright infringement of Chinese academic literature network databases, settled over 1,000 cases in the city and properly resolved potential disputes.

V. Maintaining a Sound Legal Environment for Competition to Stimulate Innovation and Creativity

People's courts continued to enhance anti-monopoly and anti-unfair competition judicial efforts. By strengthening the fundamental status of competition policies, Chinese courts maintained a sound legal environment for fair market competition, optimized the business environment, in order to make contribution to the development of a sound system of socialist market economy.

1. Improving Anti-Monopoly and Anti-Unfair Competition Judicature

In 2022, people's courts continued to improve the application rules in the field of competition, strengthened judicial trials concerning fair competition, and maintained the rule of law in market competition. The Supreme People's Court issued the *Interpretation of Several Issues concerning the Application of the Anti-Unfair Competition Law of the People's Republic of China*, which provided detailed rules regarding the Anti-Unfair Competition Law, including its General Provisions and articles on counterfeiting and confusion, false publicity, commercial defamation, and unfair competition on the internet, etc. Furthermore, the document also unified the relevant judicial standards and responded to the judicial needs arising from new fields and new business practices. The Supreme People's Court researched and drafted new judicial interpretations on anti-monopoly civil litigation, solicited public opinions, and improved judicial rules for anti-monopoly cases, while clarifying the judicial standards for determining monopolistic behaviors. The Supreme People's Court held a press conference on Chinese courts' strengthening judicial practice of anti-monopoly and anti-unfair competition, and released 10 typical cases for each category to enhance the public legal awareness for respecting and protecting fair competition. Additionally, the press conference also guided courts at all levels to punish monopolistic behaviors and maintain the market order for fair competition. People's courts at all levels enhanced judicial efforts in key fields and critical junctures such as platform economies, core technologies, medicine, and communication, and cracked down on monopolistic agreements, as well as exclusive and restrictive competition behaviors with the abuse of market dominance. Chinese courts also refined the criteria for identifying monopolistic behaviors involving internet platforms, specified the rules for determining unfair competition behaviors such as traffic hijacking and interference, and regulated and directed capital operation in healthy manner in accordance with the law. During the trial of the "Zhang Bainian" case of trademark infringement and unfair competition dispute and the Bairui Runxing case of unfair competition dispute, the Supreme People's Court clearly stated the responsibilities of sellers in disputes related to unfair competition. In the "kindergarten" case concerning horizontal monopoly agreements and the case involving the abuse of market dominance by public utility companies in relation to water supply and drainage, the Supreme People's Court responded to public concerns regarding market competition behaviors that affect people's livelihood and promptly forbade exclusive and restrictive behaviors in competition, which ensured that the public benefit from fair competition.

2. Promoting Healthy Development of the Digital Economy in Accordance with the Law

Efforts were made to explore and strengthen judicial protection of IP rights in the digital economy field, provide robust judicial services and guarantees to fully leverage the function of data, and improve the efficiency of data governance, thereby promoting high-quality development of the digital economy. Chinese courts improved hearings of cases involving data cloud storage, open-source data, data ownership, data trading, data services, and unfair competition in data markets to effectively maintain data security. In addition, research was carried out on IP rights judicial protection of data rights, as well as fair competition in the era of the digital economy, and local courts were guided to explore trial models catering to the demand of the digital economy and promote the judicial protection of innovative achievements in the digital economy. During the trial of the "web crawler platform data" case of technology secret infringement, the Supreme People's Court specified that platform data can be protected as technology secrets, which strengthened the protection of data rights and interests with competitive advantages and values created by platform operators through legitimate business operations. Jiangxi High People's Court formulated opinions on IP judicial services to safeguard the development of the digital economy and proposed 13 measures of services and guarantees. Shenzhen Intermediate People's Court of Guangdong Province issued implementation opinions on enhancing judicial protection of IP rights in the digital economy, contributing to the high-quality development of the digital economy within the city. Beijing Intellectual Property Court concluded research including "*Research on Judicial Rules regarding Competition Behaviors in New Business Practices and Models in the Digital Economy*", properly closed multiple data infringement cases, and continued to explore judicial rules where the Anti-unfair Competition Law is applied to protect data.

VI. Deepening Judicial Reforms to Improve Efficiency and Quality of IP rights Protection

The judicial reform in IP domain was deepened by people's courts, by continuing to improve the specialized trial system for IP cases, strengthening the IP litigation system, and deepening the "three-in-one" reform of IP trials. These efforts helped unify the legal application standards, enhanced diversified resolution of disputes, and improved the coordination between administrative enforcement and judicial practice, thereby enabling the comprehensive improvement of judicial protection for IP rights.

1. Promoting the Modernization of the Trial System to Boost Judicial Capacity

Led by the IP trial department of the Supreme People's Court and backed by IP divisions of local courts, China's specialized IP trial framework with 4 demonstrating IP courts and 27 IP divisions of local intermediate people's courts as the focuses, saw further improvement. The Supreme People's Court issued *Several Provisions on the Jurisdiction of Civil and Administrative Intellectual Property Cases of First Instance*, as well as its associated documents: *Notice of Issuing the Standards for Civil and Administrative Intellectual Property Cases of First Instance under Jurisdiction of Primary People's Courts*, and *Notice regarding Issues concerning the Appellate Jurisdiction of Cases Involving Disputes over Invention Patent and Other Intellectual Property Contracts*. The documents established a judicial protection system with sound jurisdictional rules, reasonably defined the trial functions of courts at four levels, and optimized the allocation of trial resources. Currently, 558 primary courts, including Internet courts, have jurisdiction over civil IP cases. Meanwhile, the Supreme People's Court continued to improve the appellate mechanism of IP cases at the national level, upgraded the retrial application procedures of IP cases, and intensified supervision and guiding to ensure the consistent application of the relevant laws and regulations. Local courts leveraged trial resources and jurisdictional mechanisms by elevating jurisdiction in accordance with the law to enable the efficient trial of IP cases and fully safeguard the rights and interests of the parties involved.

The Supreme People's Court strengthened its guiding efforts to promote the "three-in-one" trial mechanism reform of civil, administrative, and criminal IP cases across 25 high courts, 236 intermediate courts, and 275 primary courts nationwide. In particular, 10 courts have achieved full coverage of the "three-in-one" trial mechanism for IP cases within their jurisdiction. The Supreme People's Court conducted research to formulate normative documents on IP cases and issued the *Interpretation on Several Issues concerning the Application of Law in the Handling of Criminal Cases Involving Infringement on Intellectual Property Rights (Exposure Draft)* jointly with the Supreme People's Procuratorate to solicit opinions from the public. Working with the relevant departments, Heilongjiang High People's Court named the divisions which receive IP cases as IP divisions in the intermediate and primary courts, and distributed implementation plans which guidelined the practical effect of the "three-in-one" reform. High courts in provinces including Anhui, Zhejiang, Henan, and Qinghai jointly issued guiding documents with the relevant provincial procuratorates and public security departments to improve jurisdiction over criminal IP cases, which established clear procedures and sound coordination mechanisms, thereby fully implementing the "three-in-one" reform target.

Chinese courts continued to improve the diversified technical fact-finding mechanism, and improved the "Database of Technical Investigation Talents for Chinese Courts", with more than 500 technical investigators added to the Database. Additionally, the nationwide on-demand deployment and talents sharing mechanism saw continued improvements, effectively addressing the difficulties in ascertaining the facts of technology-related cases. High courts in regions such as Guangxi and Tibet introduced regulations on the engagement of technical investigators in IP cases and improved their institutional mechanisms according to local realities. Moreover, the IP tribunals in Nanjing and Suzhou fully leveraged the function of technical investigators by having them participate in the fact-finding investigation of 751 technology-related cases, conducted 66 inspections and preservations, and attend 490 trials and court hearings, with 388 technical investigation reports issued.

People's courts enhanced judicial protection of IP rights. The Supreme People's Court issued the *Opinions on Strengthening Judicial*

Protection of Intellectual Property Rights of Traditional Chinese Medicine to facilitate the inheritance and innovative development of traditional Chinese medicine. Focusing on the characteristics of IP litigation, Chinese courts conducted researches to formulate specialized procedures law for IP lawsuits. Efforts were made to curb the abuse of rights and strengthen the protection of rights holders through specialized research on regulating malicious IP litigation and the accurate application of punitive damages. Shanghai High People's Court issued opinions on handling IP cases involving small amounts to optimize and adjust the procedures for IP litigation and try simple cases quickly and tough ones delicately. Guidelines for the application of punitive damages were drafted or issued by high courts and intermediate courts in Beijing, Shandong, Guangdong, XPCC, Inner Mongolia, and other regions, with typical cases published to promote the accurate implementation of the punitive damages system in accordance with the law.

2. Contributing to the Building of an Overarching IP Protection Framework

Chinese courts continued to improve the coordination between judicial trials and administrative law enforcement to enable the unification of judicial and enforcement standards. The Supreme People's Court, jointly with government departments including the

Supreme People's Procuratorate, Ministry of Agriculture and Rural Affairs, Ministry of Commerce, Ministry of Culture and Tourism, State Administration for Market Regulation, China National Intellectual Property Administration, and National Administration of Traditional Chinese Medicine, improved coordination mechanisms and promoted institutional exchanges, data exchange, and information sharing. Additionally, the Supreme People's Court released the *Opinions on Strengthening the Alignment between Anthorities in the Identificating of Intellectual Property Rights* jointly with departments including China National Intellectual Property Administration and the Supreme People's Procuratorate to deepen cooperation between law enforcement departments and judicial organs in the field of IP identification. The Supreme People's Court and China National Intellectual Property Administration co-released the *Opinions on Strengthening the Coordinated Protection of Intellectual Property*, including 13 specific measures to improve the coordination between administrative protection and judicial protection of IP rights. The High People's Court of Shaanxi Province led the establishment of the Qinchuangyuan Intellectual Property Judicial Protection Center, involving 13 provincial-level government organs and academic institutions. The Center features a joint meeting system and offers a platform for cooperation. Guangzhou Intellectual Property Court and Shanghai Intellectual Property Court worked with China National

Intellectual Property Administration to explore the synchronization of administrative patent re-examination and infringement disputes hearings, shortening the trial period of patent infringement cases to improve patent protection.

Chinese courts accelerated the building of a diversified settlement mechanism for IP disputes, fully implemented the "head office to head office" working mechanism for the online connection between litigations and mediations, improved the system for the judicial confirmation of administrative mediation agreements, and built a joint force for protecting IP rights. Mediation organizations focusing on IP cases achieved full coverage in 30 regions across the country, with continued growth in the number of mediation organizations and mediators. People's courts entrusted more than 90,000 IP disputes to pre-litigation mediation organizations, with a success rate of over 80%, effectively resolving IP disputes in China. The Supreme People's Court intensified communication with departments including the National Copyright Administration, China Writers Association, and China Federation of Literary and Art Circles to promote the establishment of a "head office to head office" mechanism for the online connection between litigations and mediations in the field of copyright protection. Notably, the High People's Court of Hebei Province and Hebei Provincial Admiration for Market Regulation signed the *Memorandum of Cooperation on the Judicial Confirmation of Administrative Mediation Agreements for Intellectual Property Disputes*, which facilitated the resolution of 5 patent disputes through the mechanism. Courts in Shandong province handled 146 cases involving the judicial confirmation of administrative mediation agreements for IPRs disputes. The High People's Court of Liaoning Province and the Liaoning Intellectual Property Office, co-issued the *Notice on Establishing a Mechanism for the Online Connection between Litigations and Mediations Involving Intellectual Property Disputes*. After 11 mediation organizations were set up, 110 mediators stationed and successfully mediated 2,834 IP disputes, a success rate of 96.29%. Heilongjiang High People's Court and the Department of Justice of Heilongjiang Province co-founded an intellectual property arbitration court and issued the *Notice on Properly Handling Arbitration Preservation Cases in Accordance with the Law*, which facilitated the integration of litigation, arbitration, and mediation, while strengthening well-coordinated governance.

The Supreme People's Court endeavored to build regional mechanisms for IP protection, strengthen the development of IP integrity systems, and expand the promotion of the rule of law for the judicial protection of IP. The Court continued to guide relative courts to empower the coordinated development of the Beijing-

Tianjin-Hebei region, the development of the Yangtze River Economic Belt, the integrated development of the Yangtze River Delta, the building of the Guangdong-Hong Kong-Macao Greater Bay Area, the full revitalization of Northeast China, the building of the Hainan Free Trade Port, and the development of the Chengdu-Chongqing Economic Circle, thereby enabling well-coordinated regional innovation. The high people's courts of Hunan, Hubei, and Jiangxi province established a cooperative working mechanism for trials in city clusters along the middle reaches of the Yangtze River. Under their guidance, intermediate courts in cities including Yueyang, Xianning, and Jiujiang signed cross-regional IP protection agreements with the competent market regulation departments to explore solutions to new challenges in cross-regional, large-scale, and collective IP infringement. The high people's courts of Sichuan province and Chongqing municipality jointly held the 2022 Sichuan-Chongqing Intellectual Property Protection Seminar to enable the integrated protection of IP rights in both regions. Beijing Intellectual Property Court, the No.3 Intermediate Court of Tianjin, and the Intermediate Court of Xiong'an New Area signed the *Cooperation Framework Agreement on Strengthening Judicial Protection of Intellectual Property*, a move that promoted cooperation including talent training, trial collaboration, and experience sharing. The Intellectual Property Court of the Hainan Free Trade Port sent judicial recommendations to Hainan Administration for Market Regulation and the Intellectual Property Office of Hainan Province, publicly listing 12 individuals involved in 9 criminal cases of IP infringement as serious violators of IP laws. The Intermediate Court of Dalian city of Liaoning Province sent judicial recommendations to the local administration for market regulation, publicly disclosing the information of 4 entities involved in intentional IP infringement. The People's Court of Binhai New Area of Tianjin adopted new regulations to report persons subject to execution in IP cases who failed to fulfill their obligations to departments for market regulation, financial institutions, and industry associations. During Intellectual Property Promotion Week, the Supreme People's Court held a press conference and planned a series of events to showcase the achievements of Chinese courts in providing judicial protection for IPRs from all angles, perspectives and depths. Courts in regions including Jilin, Gansu, Qinghai, Ningxia, and XPCC released well-planned typical cases and conducted events such as public hearings and public enforcement to encourage the general public to respect and protect IP rights.

VII. Upholding the Legal Equality in IP rights Protection and Promoting International Communication and Cooperation

Chinese courts made greater efforts to establish China as a preferred venue for international IP litigation, properly tried major IP disputes related to international trade, and created an open, transparent judicial environment, as well as a sound market environment for fair competition, thereby contributing to a greater degree of opening up. In 2022, Chinese courts concluded nearly 9,000 IP cases of first instance involving foreign parties. During the trial of administrative dispute case between Manolo Blahnik and China National Intellectual Property Administration regarding the invalidity of trademark rights, the Supreme People's Court equally protected the prior rights of the foreign party and received a letter of appreciation from the Spanish Embassy in China. Courts in Jiangsu newly accepted 527 IP cases involving foreign parties, with a trademark infringement and unfair competition dispute involving a well-known foreign brand concluded. In that case, punitive damages were awarded in accordance with the law, and the foreign rights holder's claim for compensation of 50 million yuan was upheld. In Guangdong, courts resolved a series of standard essential patent disputes involving foreign parties and assisted the parties in reaching global package settlement via mediation. The Primary People's Court of Siming in Xiamen, Fujian Province, and the International Commercial Mediation Center for Belt and Road Initiative established the Intellectual Property Mediation Room of the Maritime Silk Road Central Legal District, expanding the channel for mediating IP disputes involving foreign parties jointly.

Committed to building a community with a shared future for humanity, Chinese courts actively engaged in global IP governance under the framework of the WIPO, deepened judicial IP cooperation with other nations and regions, and pushed for the improvement of international rules and standards on IP rights. The Supreme People's Court sent judges to participate in the Third China-ASEAN Justice Forum and the Fourth Session for the China-Singapore Supreme Courts Joint Working Group, and co-organized with the European Union the Seminar on Specialized Litigation Procedures for IP Cases. Judges were also sent to attend conferences including the 2022 WIPO Intellectual Property Judges Forum, the WIPO Assemblies Side Event: WIPO ADR for IPOs and Courts, the Fifteenth Session of the Advisory Committee on Enforcement (ACE), as well as the 13th Meeting of the Russia-China Working Group on Cooperation in Protection of IPRs, which was organized by the Ministry of Commerce of China. In addition, the Supreme People's Court co-organized the Seminar on the Legal Application and Judicial Cooperation in IP Cases between China's Mainland and Hong Kong jointly with the HKSAR Department of Justice, participated in the drafting of the China chapter of the WIPO *International Patent Case Management Judicial Guide*, and offered advanced courses through the WIPO Distance Learning Courses in Chinese. Fujian High People's Court and the WIPO Arbitration and Mediation Center signed the *Agreement on Strengthening Communication and Cooperation on Alternative Dispute Resolution for Intellectual Property Rights* and formulated the corresponding coordination and working mechanisms.

VIII. Leveraging the Guiding Role of Party Building to Build a First-Class Judicial Team

Committed to the political development of the Party, Chinese courts strengthened political loyalty, engaged in impartial and honest judicial practices, and endeavored to build an IP trial team of law and technology-savvy professionals with political integrity, big-picture thinking, and a global outlook.

The 20th National Congress of the Communist Party of China is a meeting of great importance. It takes place at a critical time as the entire Party and the Chinese people of all ethnic groups embark on a new journey to build China into a modern socialist country in all respects and advance toward the Second Centenary Goal. The 20th National Congress draws a grand blueprint for advancing the great rejuvenation of the Chinese nation on all fronts through Chinese modernization, while making arrangements for improving the legal protection of IP rights. Chinese courts adhered to the absolute leadership of the Party on judicial work concerning IP. Having gained a deep understanding of the decisive significance of establishing Comrade Xi Jinping's core position on the Party Central Committee and in the Party as a whole and establishing the guiding role of Xi Jinping Thought on Socialism with Chinese Characteristics for a New Era, Chinese courts endeavored to fully study, understand, and implement the guiding principles from the 20th National Congress. They have relied on Xi Jinping Thought on Socialism with Chinese Characteristics for a New Era to enhance cohesion and forge the judicial soul. Upholding Xi Jinping Thought on the Rule of Law in judicial practices involving IP, Chinese courts extensively conducted the "Two Establishments" theme education program to consolidate the progress made in learning the Party's history and the education and rectification of political and legal teams. Furthermore, Chinese courts continued to promote the high-quality development of judicial work on IP.

Chinese courts strictly adhered to stringent prohibitions such as the "Three Provisions" and the "Ten Prohibitions" for court staff members in the new era. In 2022, Chinese courts implemented the "list of prohibited industries" for close relatives and regulated post-employment behaviors of court staff members, fully implemented the judicial accountability system, standardized the exercise of judicial power, and established the mechanism for the exercise of judicial power and supervision in the field of IP rights, thereby guaranteeing impartial and honest judicial practices. Chinese courts continued to intensify education and training in an effort to enhance the political, theoretical, and practical competence of court staff members, carry forward their fighting spirit and build up their fighting ability. The Supreme People's Court held a press conference on the new judicial interpretations and judicial policies pertaining to IP rights to facilitate the accurate application of laws by local courts. In addition, the Court mobilized efforts to compile the IP and competition volume of the *Application of the Civil Code of the People's Republic of China* and compiled summaries of judicial opinions to guide trial practices. The high people's courts of Sichuan and Chongqing jointly organized a training course on judicial protection of IP with the people's procuratorates. Under their guidance, Chengdu Intermediate People's Court and Chongqing No. 1 Intermediate People's Court co-hosted a forum for IP judges. The High People's Court of Yunnan Province and the Yunnan Administration for Market Regulation jointly held a training course on administrative enforcement and judicial protection of IP rights to broaden the judicial horizons of IP judges. Focusing on the characteristics of border port cities, Dandong Intermediate People's Court of Liaoning Province organized trainings with the Dandong Customs District to enhance trial officials' knowledge of international brand protection.

Conclusion

2023 marks the first year for fully implementing the guiding principles of the 20th National Congress of the Communist Party of China. In IP trials, Chinese courts will continue to follow the guidance of Xi Jinping Thought on Socialism with Chinese Characteristics for a New Era, thoroughly implement the guiding principles from the Party's 20th National Congress and the first and second plenary sessions of the 20th Central Committee. Chinese courts will practice Xi Jinping Thought on the Rule of Law across the board and gain a deep understanding of the decisive significance of establishing Comrade Xi Jinping's core position on the Party Central Committee and in the Party as a whole and establishing the guiding role of Xi Jinping Thought on Socialism with Chinese Characteristics for a New Era. Chinese courts will enhance their consciousness of the need to maintain political integrity, think in big-picture terms, follow the leadership core, and keep in alignment with the central Party leadership. Chinese courts will stay confident in the path, theory, system, and culture of socialism with Chinese characteristics, uphold Comrade Xi Jinping's core position on the Party Central Committee and in the Party as a whole and uphold the Central Committee's authority and its centralized, unified leadership. Under the absolute leadership of the Party, Chinese courts will adhere resolutely to the path of socialist rule of law with Chinese characteristics and endeavor to ensure that the people perceive fairness and justice in every judicial case. Chinese courts will strive to increase their political awareness, consider the big picture, enhance judicial fairness and efficiency, prioritize self-discipline and team building, and provide impartial judicial services to the people on a consistent basis. This year, Chinese courts will " strengthen legal protection of intellectual property rights in order to establish a foundational system for all-around innovation" and create an open, fair, just and non-discriminatory environment for the development of science and technology, as well as a world-class business environment that is market-oriented, law-based, and internationalized, thereby contributing to the start of the construction of a fully modern socialist country.